797,885 Books
are available to read at

Forgotten Books

www.ForgottenBooks.com

Forgotten Books' App
Available for mobile, tablet & eReader

ISBN 978-1-331-06253-0
PIBN 10139895

This book is a reproduction of an important historical work. Forgotten Books uses state-of-the-art technology to digitally reconstruct the work, preserving the original format whilst repairing imperfections present in the aged copy. In rare cases, an imperfection in the original, such as a blemish or missing page, may be replicated in our edition. We do, however, repair the vast majority of imperfections successfully; any imperfections that remain are intentionally left to preserve the state of such historical works.

Forgotten Books is a registered trademark of FB &c Ltd.
Copyright © 2017 FB &c Ltd.
FB &c Ltd, Dalton House, 60 Windsor Avenue, London, SW19 2RR.
Company number 08720141. Registered in England and Wales.

For support please visit www.forgottenbooks.com

1 MONTH OF FREE READING

at

www.ForgottenBooks.com

By purchasing this book you are eligible for one month membership to ForgottenBooks.com, giving you unlimited access to our entire collection of over 700,000 titles via our web site and mobile apps.

To claim your free month visit: www.forgottenbooks.com/free139895

* Offer is valid for 45 days from date of purchase. Terms and conditions apply.

English
Français
Deutsche
Italiano
Español
Português

www.forgottenbooks.com

Mythology Photography **Fiction** Fishing Christianity **Art** Cooking Essays Buddhism Freemasonry Medicine **Biology** Music **Ancient Egypt** Evolution Carpentry Physics Dance Geology **Mathematics** Fitness Shakespeare **Folklore** Yoga Marketing **Confidence** Immortality Biographies Poetry **Psychology** Witchcraft Electronics Chemistry History **Law** Accounting **Philosophy** Anthropology Alchemy Drama Quantum Mechanics Atheism Sexual Health **Ancient History Entrepreneurship** Languages Sport Paleontology Needlework Islam **Metaphysics** Investment Archaeology Parenting Statistics Criminology **Motivational**

Notes of a Staff Officer

of our

First New Jersey Brigade

on the

Seven Day's Battle on the Peninsula in 1862

by

E. Burd Grubb

Brevet Brigadier General U. S. Volunteers

Moorestown, N. J.
MOORESTOWN PPINTING CO.
1910.

The Seven Day's Battle on the Peninsula as Seen by a Lieutenant on the Staff

Camille Baquet, Esq.,
  Historian of First New Jersey Brigade,
    Elizabeth, N. J.
Dear Sir:

In accordance with your request I give you herewith my recollections of the Battle of Gaines' Mills. In order to give a minute description of this battle, it may be well to describe where the New Jersey Brigade started from to go into it, and how it came to be where it did start from.

The Brigade had been at the village of Mechanicsville about three and a half miles from Richmond on the northern side of the Chickahominy during the latter part of the month of May. It was moved up from Mechanicsville about a mile and a half west up the Chickahominy near the Meadow Bridge, but was not on picket at that bridge when Fitzhugh Lee's cavalry attacked the picket of the United States Cavalry commanded by Captain Royal and killed a number of his men and desperately wounded that officer. Captain Royal was well known in Burlington, New Jersey, he having married a sister of Admiral John Howell of that city.

The brigade was withdrawn soon after that and moved down the Chickahominy taking the road on top of the northern ridge and stopping near Dr. Gaines' house.

On the 31st of May the brigade was under orders to move at a moment's notice and the Battle of Fair Oaks was in progress on the southern side of the river. Part of it could be seen and a good deal of it heard.

On the morning of the first of June the brigade moved down across the Chickahominy and out on the battle field of Fair Oaks. General Taylor informed me that we had been held in reserve through the morning and were considered the support of the second line. We were not engaged because the fight was practically over before we reached the field, but Captain George Wood, whose mother lived next to my father's house in Burlington and who was captain in a Pennsylvania regiment, was carried by and spoke to me while I was sitting on my horse with General Taylor at the edge of the battle field. Captain Wood was shot through the leg. The brigade was encamped on this battle field along the eastern side of the road running to Richmond, having crossed on what was known as the Grapevine Bridge, across the Chickahominy, and while there I visited the Second Brigade, many of whom, particularly in the Fifth Regiment, came from Burlington. George Burling, afterwards Gen. Burling, commanded a regiment. They had had a very desperate fight and many of them had been killed and wounded. They were camped directly on the spot where they had fought, and for many reasons it was the most disagreeable camp I ever saw, dead men and dead horses having been only covered with perhaps six inches or a foot of earth and the stench and the flies exceeded anything I ever saw before or since. We remained here until the morning of the 27th of June. All through the afternoon of the 26th up to nine o'clock that night there had been a heavy battle raging at and around Mechanicsville and the roar of the guns and the flashes of the shells had been very continuous. Early in the morning of the 27th the brigade was moved down with the rest of Slocum's division near the Grapevine Bridge and over the small hill from which the north side of the Chickahominy River could be very well seen.

It is my recollection that the tents which were of course shelter tents, and the knap-sacks of all the brigade, were left in the camp when we moved out that morning and the reason I think so is because I was in charge of the detail which buried the knap-sacks of the entire Fourth Regiment which were in their camp when we returned late on the night of the 27th after the battle. These knap-sacks were buried on the morning of the 28th of June, 1862, and while I have never been at the place since, although I have visited the battle field of Gaines' Mills twice, I have always thought that I could find this place. If the members of the Fourth Regiment have not already done so, of this I do not know.

About eight o'clock in the morning General Taylor directed me to go over the river and get some idea of the topography of the ground upon which we would probably fight. After crossing the river, riding across, I went to the westward, crossing a field or two, and came to a barn on the top of which were some signal officers, one of whom I knew, he being from my own regiment. He asked me to come up on top of the barn, and I climbed up and from there about half a mile away through a small gap in the woods, I watched a solid column of the enemy passing from left to right, until I was sure that a very heavy body of infantry was making that movement,I then went to the northwestward until I came to our line of battle. The men were lying down along the edge of the pine woods and so far as I saw, there was no rifle pit or attempt of any shelter of that kind, I rode along for certainly the length of the entire division and got a fair idea of the lay of the land, and I saw a place which has considerable to do with my account of this battle. It was a swale or shallow ravine possibly, where it came through the pine woods, about six feet deep and one hundred feet wide. On the northwest side of it there was a peach orchard and high grass and from the configuration of the country, I judged that the swale was formed from the water wash through that orchard towards the Chickahominy. There was no creek or rivulet going through it, but there was quite a deep ditch running along in the fields to the eastward perpendicular to the direction of the swale. Our line of battle was not in the ditch but considerably to the westward of it, say one hundred and fifty yards, I do not remember what troops were there, but I think that at least some of them were Regulars. My reason for thinking so is because I spoke to and saw regular officers whom I knew. The line of battle was not extended across this swale when I saw it in the morning, nor was it in the afternoon when I saw it again. I extended my observations along the line of battle for probably a mile to which this swale was nearly a central point. I made careful observations because I could not tell where our brigade would go in. I made a pencil sketch of the line as it appeared to me and returned to General Taylor with as much information as I could give him together with the sketch. The swale and ditch were marked upon the sketch as was also the barn where the signal officers were, and the general direction and the distance from the bridge head as near as I could give it. I do not know why it occurred to me that the course of the brigade should be to the left after we crossed the bridge, but it was so, and the reason I did think so was because I saw immediately that that was the weakest part of our line of battle.

About two o'clock in the afternoon we had not yet crossed the bridge. It will be remembered that one of the names of this battle of Gaines' Mills, is the "noiseless battle." A four o'clock in the afternoon there were nearly sixty thousand men engaged, having a great number of cannon, firing an immense number of cartridges, (of course at that time loaded with black noisy powder) and it is a fact that persons within two miles of that battle never heard a sound of it. Ordinarily the noise of that battle would easily have been heard for fifty miles.

I remember afterwards that although the smoke of the guns and of the musketry and the bursting of the shells in the air was distinctly visible to all of us; yet there was exceedingly little or no noise where we were until after we crossed the bridge, although we were within three-quarters of a mile from where the battle was going on.

I think there are only one or two occasions in the history of the world in which such peculiar conditions of the atmosphere existed at the time of battle. About three o'clock one of General Slocum's aides came to General Taylor with orders to cross the bridge at once, we moved down and crossed, and were directed to move obliquely to the left and take position in a large field which was a clover field, in echelon. The battalions were closed in mass on the centre with intervals of one hundred and twenty paces between the battalions. The Fourth Regiment was the left rear echelon; the Third was the next; then the Second; then the First. The field was a very large one and sloped both ways, first the rise from the river to the top of it, then a slope towards the pine woods which I have spoken of on the northern side. In forming the echelon, all the brigade passed over the crest of the hill. As soon as the brigade was in this position General Taylor ordered arms in place rest.

In front of us and about five hundred yards away there was going on a very severe battle, and many bullets came up from the woods and some cannon balls and shells. In a few moments the General sent orders to the brigade to lie down. Just as we came into position, a brigade which had been fighting in the woods right in front of us and which contained Duryea's Regiment of Zouaves of New York, fell back out of the woods not in very much disorder, but breaking both to the right and left. Their place was taken by Sykes' Brigade of the regular army which passed into their place coming from the left and which went into position just about the time that our men lay down on the hill. The regulars took up a fight which commenced to rage again with great fury; their line pressed into the woods and disappeared from our sight. The bullets commenced to come out of the woods and come in where we were in a very disagreeable manner, which I distinctly remember, as I sat on my horse with much more apparent coolness than I really felt, alongside of the General who certainly was very cool. In a few moments a very great many wounded men began to come back from the woods, some being carried, some being assisted, and some limping back themselves; and before very long an aide of General Slocum's came to General Taylor and ordered him to put his brigade in line of battle and advance. At this moment an incident occurred of which I was personally cognizant and part of which I was an eye witness to. I may digress here for a moment, and say that on the crest of the hill of which I have spoken and which we passed, lying between the Fourth and the Third Regiments, was a battery of seven machine guns, the first that were ever tried in battle, I believe, and the only ones I think at that time in any army of the world. They were called the "Union Coffee Mill Guns" and consisted of a single rifle barrel with an arrangement like a hopper at the butt of the barrel, into which cartridges were put, and the turning of a crank did the rest. I have also called to mind the fact that at the battle of Gaines' Mills the first New Jersey Brigade used a cartridge in which the powder and ball were enclosed together in some inflammable paper, it not being necessary to bite the cartridge but merely to put it in the rifle and ram down. I do not think they were ever used after the Peninsula Campaign, but the brigade was furnished with from sixty to eighty of these cartridges per man at the battle of Gaines' Mills, I think the "Union Coffee Mill Guns" had this same kind of a cartridge, but I am not sure of this.

Sergeant Dalzell of the Third New Jersey Regiment in the writhings of this battle was for a time in charge of this battery and I think that finally all the guns were lost. The reason that I speak about this battery so particularly is because it was at a trial of these machine guns some weeks previous at which I was present, by General Taylor's orders, I met for the first time the two French officers now known as the Comte de Paris, the Bourbon Pretender to the throne of France, and his cousin the Duke de Chartres. These officers I subsequently met on several occasions when I was sent with messages from General Taylor to General McClellan while the brigade occupied the extreme right of the army above Mechanicsville near the Meadow Bridge. I knew them by sight and from introduction and they did not very much resemble each other.

Immediately after General Slocum's aide had given orders to General Taylor to advance his brigade and before the brigade had gotten into line of battle from the massed formation, an officer riding very fast and coming down the line from the east rode up to General Taylor and commenced speaking to him very rapidly in French (both of these officers whom I have mentioned spoke English perfectly well). General Taylor neither spoke nor understood French, and he turned to me and said: "Who the devil is this, and what is he talking about?" I said to him: "This is the Comte de Paris serving on General McClellan's staff, and he has come to you by General Porter's orders under which you are to give him one of our regiments." General Taylor said to me. "Do you know him?" I said, "Yes, sir, I do." He said: "Very well, then give him the Fourth Regiment and go and see where he puts it and come back and report." These last few words saved me a trip to Libby Prison. We started up at once after the Fourth Regiment where we arrived in a few jumps of our horses. The French officer was a good deal excited. He was a young man probably about twenty-five or six years of age. I do not think that he said anything to me as we were riding, but I do remember that his horse shied at a dead man who lay in our way and very nearly threw him over his head. Arrived at the Fourth Regiment whose Colonel Simpson, a West Point officer, was just beginning to form his line of battle. I introduced him. Colonel Simpson spoke French very well and their conversation was in French. I understood it and heard him tell Col. Simpson just what I had told General Taylor and he said that if Col. Simpson would get his regiment in columns of fours he would conduct him where he wanted to go. The regiment was put into columns of fours and went off to the left front with Col. Simpson, the French officer and myself riding at the head of it, Col. Simpson on the left of us and the French officer between us. We had not gone far before I saw that we were approaching the swale that I have spoken of before, and soon we arrived at it. To my great surprise there was no more line of battle there than there was in the morning, although there was a very heavy battle going on on the right on the eastern side of this swale. My recollection is that there was not much going on on the left or western side, but I cannot say that I remember distinctly about that. At the mouth of this swale, apparently waiting for the Fourth Regiment, was the Eleventh Pennsylvania Regiment also in columns and also apparently under the orders of this French officer; for as soon as the Fourth came up both regiments moved off together through this swale. The rest of this is soon told. The last I saw of the French officer and Col. Simpson and the right of that regiment was a swarm of grey coated soldiers with their rifles in their hands within no more than thirty yards from us, and with General Taylor's words in my ears to "Come back and report," I lay flat down on my horse, put both spurs to him and did so. I rode up the line until I came to some wounded soldiers of the Third Regiment, and right here I saw Col. Tucker of the Second Regiment carried out of the woods and put on a stretcher and then shot dead after he was on the stretcher. I asked some of the Third men where General Taylor was, and they said "With the Third Regiment," of which regiment he had been colonel before he was promoted. I dismounted and tied my horse to a little mulberry tree at the edge of the woods and to which tree General Taylor's horse was also tied, and which tree is still alive, or was so within the last four years, as I saw it. I then went up through the woods about one hundred and fifty yards and came upon the line of battle and soon found General Taylor parading up and down the line like a wounded lion and in the midst of one of the most terrible battles I ever saw.

As soon as I came close to him and he saw me he said: "Where is the Fourth?" I said: "Gone to Richmond, sir." I shall never forget how the old fellow's eyes glared as with his sword in his hand, he turned to me and said: "Young man, this is no place for levity." I said: "They are captured, every man of them." He said: "My God, My God," and fairly wrung his hands.

Now this is an incident of the capture of the Fourth Regiment as witnessed and participated in by a staff officer. The identity of the French officer who conducted the Fourth Regiment into the woods where it was lost has been a subject of question ever since.

Colonel Simpson in his report of the battle and his capture mentions the name of the Duke de Charteres as having been his conductor.

When I joined General Taylor he was near the left of the companies of the Third Regiment; the smoke was so thick that it was impossible to see twenty yards. The afternoon was very hot and the air close, and probably the peculiar condition of the atmosphere of which I have spoken had something to do with it, for I never saw smoke so thick in any battle as it was at Gaines' Mills.

The firing of the enemy in our front was very constant, rapid, and heavy, and while a good many of our men were being hit it appeared to me that the bullets went high and the bark and the chips fell off the trees over our heads. All of the men of the Third Regiment were lying down on the ground loading and firing from that position and the same was true of the First and Second Regiments who were on the right of the Third. The first and only order that General Taylor gave me after I joined him in the woods was given within two or three minutes after I came up to him and after my report of the Fourth Regiment which I have detailed above. He said: "Those men are not firing at anything. It is too thick to see. Go to the regiments and give the order to cease firing and let the smoke rise." I went along the line, gave the order to every officer whom I saw—captains, lieutenants, and field officers. There were a great many of the poor fellows dead and hurt, and my dear cousin, Penrose Buckley, Captain of Company C, of the Third Regiment, with whom I had enlisted in May, 1861, was lying on the ground among his men, several of whom were dead and a number wounded, and he was pressing a bloody handkerchief to his left hip as I passed along. I said to him: "How is it with you, Penn?" and he said: "Not bad, Ned, only a buck shot in my hip." That is the last I ever saw of him. He was shot through the lungs a few minutes afterwards and lay on that spot four days in agony and died there. Before this last mortal wound he had a hand to hand encounter with two of the enemy, one of whom he killed, and the other shot him through the lungs. This is the testimony of John Stewart, Sergeant of Company C, who was lying on the ground beside him with his right arm shot off at the wrist, and who is still living at this day. After having communicated the order to fire I returned along the line looking for General Taylor, as I reached about the centre of the Third Regiment the smoke had risen from the ground as a curtain rolls up slowly and there was no firing on the part of the enemy, our men doubtless glad to be relieved from their cramped positions, arose from the ground, some on their knees, and some standing erect peering through the smoke.

As we know now that the enemy were in the sunken road which passed through the woods parallel with the line of the brigade and where undoubtedly our line of battle should have been formed in the morning. This sunken road was deep enough to cover a man to his arm pits and therefore only the head and shoulders of the enemy were above the level of the ground, and the enemy was distant only about forty-five yards when what I am speaking of occurred. I have paced the distance more than once since on that spot and I believe this to be accurate.

Both General Taylor and I distinctly heard the clear order, "Aim," come out of the smoke at the front, and instantly the order, "Fire." The volley that fell upon the brigade was the most withering I ever saw delivered, for the men were totally unprepared for it. Under that volley, the New Jersey Brigade broke all to pieces I do not know whether before this there was any break in the line of battle to the left of the New Jersey Brigade. History is somewhat misty about this, but I do know that the brigade fell back in great disorder upon receiving this volley.

General Taylor and several of the officers attempted to rally the men, but this was impossible. The General said to me: "We must get in front of them. Where's my horse?" It happened that I knew where his horse was for I had tied my own beast to the same mulberry tree and he was no more than fifty or sixty yards from where we were. James Morrow, of Company C, Third Regiment, who is still living, helped me to find these horses, and directly at the edge of the woods and right in the midst of the retiring brigade Gen. Taylor ordered me to get in front of the men, which would be to the rear, for he was coming back to rally them. We had gone but a few steps when we came to a ditch which I have spoken of previously and my horse, which was the black stallion so well known to our brigade, cleared the ditch easily at one bound, Gen. Taylor's horse balked just on the edge of it and Gen. Taylor very nearly went over his head. Seeing that the horse would not leap, I dismounted, went through the ditch and then led him up on the other side, upon which Gen. Taylor put spurs to his horse and galloped off swinging his sword and calling to his men to rally.

One of the curious incidents of my life happened just here My horse was very much excited by the noise and confusion, and just as I put one foot in the stirrup he swung around so that I had great difficulty in getting the other leg up, finally I did so and was just starting to rejoin Gen. Taylor when a very tall and handsome young man came to me, and put his hand on the pommel of my saddle, he had in his other hand a National Regimental color. The lower part of his face and his chest was covered with blood. He said to me: "I am hit so hard that I don't think I can go any further, so I turn this over to you." I took the colors, put my horse to full run, went through the crowd of retreating men and found Gen. Taylor, who was forming a line about a quarter of a mile in the rear of where we had been fighting, and found a small patch of the Second Regiment, which was the nucleus around which that Regiment was rallying, and gave the colors to them.

The curious part of this matter is that I do not remember that I ever had occasion to mention this incident in public until the year 1888, when I was Department Commander of the G. A. R. in

New Jersey, and at a Camp Fire in Freehold in the Opera House before a very large audience and an attentive one, I related it. Upon stating just as I have now, and saying that I turned those colors over finally to the rallying regiment, a tall, white-haired man with a long, drooping white moustache rising from the centre of the audience said: "That is exactly true, I am the man, and here is the wound," and drawing aside his moustache he showed that his lips had been almost entirely cut off which was the wound of which I have spoken and he was the color bearer of our Second Regiment, who had turned the colors over to me at the Battle of Gaines' Mills. An account of this curious incident was published in the Freehold papers the following day.

As the brigade retreated from the woods we saw a melancholy sight of our guns of the artillery of our division being captured, and we also had a glimpse of the rushing to and fro of a small body of cavalry which is known to be Rush's Lancers, Sixth Pennsylvania Cavalry. Twenty-one of those guns were lost right there, and I wish to say that our brigade was not at any time placed in support of these guns directly.

The last I saw of the Union Coffee Mills guns they were in a mass together in a little rise of the ground about two hundred yards back of our line and this was when we were retreating. I have always understood here that Sergeant Dalzell, who was the color bearer of the Third Regiment, was with these guns at that time

After returning the colors to a group of the Second Regiment which was the nucleus of the new line and which line was forming very rapidly, for the men were not running away in a panic at all, and after Gen. Taylor got in front of them and called them to rally, they did rally and at once. It was then getting quite dusk and on the right of our brigade there came up a brigade from the direction of the Chickahominy and this I found to be Gen. Meagher's Irish Brigade. This brigade went into position of the right of our line, and I want to say that our line was formed before that brigade came up, and of this I am positive.

While our line was forming, men came in from the front and took position, regardless of what regiment they belonged and in that line there were a great many men of other regiments besides the Jersey Regiments. Gen. Taylor told me to go to the left and help anybody form the line down to the river, and this I did. Assisting several general officers whose names I did not know, and about dark there was quite a good line formed. The left of which extended almost to the river if not quite there. There were a few pieces of artillery in this line on the left and some few cavalry. The enemy came out of the woods immediately after the brigade retreated through the woods, a very solid, good formation, but after taking the guns which I have spoken of, for some extraordinary reason they did not come on any farther, and why I have never been able to ascertain from any account of this battle that I have ever read. There was no military reason that any one can see why a charge by the enemy along the line, or at any part of it, after Gen. Porter's line of battle was broken should not have been entirely and absolutely successful.

There is no question that our brigade and others would have fought on that last line, but I think that it would have been a forlorn hope. The battle was totally lost and every man knew it.

The enemy did not advance, and after dark the troops commenced to retire across the bridges in our rear. These bridges were small, frail things not much wider than four men could march abreast.

In the rear of the entire left of the new line of which I spoke, there was only one of them. The orders to withdraw our brigade came to General Taylor about quarter of nine o'clock. The enemy had been firing slowly with artillery and undoubtedly endeavoring to strike the bridges and many of their shot came close to the bridge heads, but I do not think that any of them struck the bridge itself.

Just at nine o'clock as the Third Regiment was going over the bridge and the General and myself were riding with it, just before we came to the bridge head Lieutenant Howell of Company I, of the Third Regiment, who was one of my dearest personal friends, came out of the ranks and shook hands with me saying how glad he was that we were both alive. He walked a few paces and turned there to say something else to me or to some of his company, and a round shot that was fired by the enemy's gun struck him full in the breast and literally tore him to pieces.

The brigade crossed the bridge and returned to its camp which they left in the morning not far from the Fair Oaks battlefield which it reached about ten o'clock that night. This was one of the most sorrowful nights that I ever remember. We had lost a great battle, which every man and officer knew should never have been fought in that way, and at that place, and every one of us lost dear friends and companions and what was worse their mangled bodies were at the tender mercy of the enemy. Only a few wounded men escaped and what few we did get away were taken to the field hospital at Savage Station and fell into the hands of the enemy there. This battle was a stupendous military error from beginning to end. History shows now and our military leaders should have known then, that, after the battle of Mechanicsville, the day before, in which the enemy suffered severe repulse, the right wing of our army should have been withdrawn that night to the south of the Chickahominy River, and under no circumstances should have been allowed to wait, in that false position in which they met the fierce assault of the forty thousand fresh troops of Stonewall Jackson, who was then coming through the valley, and was known to be coming, and who struck us hard in the place where we were without entrenchments and without support, on the afternoon of the 27th of June. Any one who reads history cannot fail to see that General McClellan's fatal mistake in his Chickahominy campaign was that he did not advance with his whole force on Richmond after he had practically won the battle of Fair Oaks.

The next morning the sorrowful duty of burying the knapsacks of the Fourth Regiment to which I have alluded, was performed, and I was detailed to see that this was done, and I did so and I think I can find the place, although I have never tried to. The next day the brigade moved to Savage Station and after a short halt moved on towards White Oak Swamp. During this halt at Savage Station many of us visited the field hospitals in which were the wounded whom we had been able to bring from the Gaines' Mills fight, and many wounded men who had been in that battle were in tents scattered around the ground of the station house, and here I paid a last farewell to many a dear friend, among them Lieutenant Wm. Evans of Company B of the Third Regiment, one of the most devoted friends of my life, who was shot through the upper part of the left lung and died within twenty-four hours after we left him. I pushed into his jacket as I said good-bye, all the money I had, not more than six or seven dollars except one silver ten cent piece, and this also I parted with near Malvern Hill as I shall relate.

When the brigade reached the first bridge from the White Oak Swamp it was halted and General Taylor was told by an aid of General Slocum's that we were to be the rear division of the army, and that he must keep himself in touch with Division Headquarters wherever they were. This order caused me to ride a great many miles, for I had two horses and they were both kept pretty busy. As we reached the bridge head, of course it was a very small bridge, there was a very heavy cannonade apparently across our front about half a mile away. I was sent to see what it was and found that the enemy had opened a battery or several batteries on a pack of our wagons which had in some way become exposed to them. The hill country was covered thickly with trees and underbrush. There were very few clearings and scarcely any high ground, and it was very difficult to see what was going on. I could see, however, that there was a great panic among the teamsters and that the wagons were being deserted, and the wagoners riding off on the mules and horses of the teams. Presently our line of skirmishers appeared facing the southwest and at that time the head of our column was facing the east, so the position was very much mixed. The skirmishers advanced towards the Rebel batteries very rapidly, and while I was looking on the batteries withdrew. I went back and reported to General Taylor and drew a diagram of what I had seen and gave it to him, and told him I was utterly unable to understand the positions, but that these were facts. An aid of General Slocum's came up with orders to cross the bridge and turn sharply to the right which would cause us to march about due south. This we did for probably a mile or more and then came to a fairly good bridge across White Oak Creek and this the brigade crossed. After crossing, the creek here ran through a ravine the sides of which were quite precipitous, the road down to the bridge on one side and up on the other being very steep. An aid of General Slocum's told General Taylor that our brigade was now the rear of the army, that there was a piece of our artillery on the north side of the creek, that he expected General Taylor to look after it when the pickets and skirmishers were withdrawn. After awhile, probably half an hour, some of the pickets commenced to come across the bridge, and having nothing to do I thought I would go acrss the bridge and see where that piece of artillery was. I found it on top of the hill about five hundred yards from the bridge in good position commanding the road. The officer in charge was a lieutenant of Williston's battery whom I knew very well. He asked me if I had any orders for him, when I said no, he said he would like to have an order.

So after a little while I went back to the brigade. The pickets and skirmishers were coming across the bridge and after a while a few of our cavalry came across and after that the pioneers commenced to destroy th bridge by hewing through the timbers. We were lying down and resting on the top of the hill on the south side of the ravine when I saw the pioneers commence to cut the bridge to pieces. I said to General Taylor: "Why that gun is over on the other side." He said, "How do you know it is?" I said: "Why I saw it half an hour ago." He used a very strong expression, pulling his moustache and told me to tell our lieutenant to "get out of that as quick as the Lord would let him." So I ran down and stopped the men from cutting the bridge, ran up the other side and told the officer of the gun what the general had said. They were all ready and sitting on their horses but had had no order to move. The enemy's skirmishers who were coming on had fired several shots at them, and I must say that I never saw a gun go down a hill more rapidly than that did. To make a long story short they got the gun over all right, and the enemy's skirmishers shot at our pioneers while they were cutting the bridge. This was a curious, but as it turned out, a very fortunate occurrence, for history shows that these were Stonewall Jackson's men, and that Jackson with a heavy force was behind them. They reported that this bridge was held strongly with artillery and infantry, and this report made such an impression upon Jackson that he did not attempt to force the passage of the creek at that place. Why he did not cross the creek at a fort about a mile further up of which he should have known, historians on both sides have never discovered; but that Jackson's delay on that occasion, at that spot and his counter march gave McClellan the opportunity to withdraw his armies successfully to Malvern Hill, is the opinion of all authorities whom I have read upon the subject.

This was about two o'clock in the afternoon, it must be remembered that this was when the days were long and also very hot. In half an hour we received orders to march and move south along the White Oak road towards Charles City crossroads. After marching about two miles we were halted and the men were directed to rest along the east side of the road which was well wooded on the east side, and on the west side were several quite large clearings. I am sure that General Taylor was not informed that we were occupying the line of battle, and I am sure that General Torbert, who was then colonel of the First Regiment, did not know this until several years after, but it is a fact that we were a part of the line and an exceedingly important part. While we were lying down along the edge of the road an aid of General Slocum's rode by and told General Taylor that General Slocum's headquarters were in the field on the left or east side of the road about five hundred yards ahead of us, and that was all he said to him, for I heard it, and he then rode away. In about fifteen minutes the enemy opened with about sixty pieces of artillery, firing across the road in front of us and gradually increasing the rapidity of the firing until it was the most tremendous cannonade I had ever heard. No enemy was visible to us anywhere, the smoke of those guns came over the edge of the woods probably eight hundred yards from the road, and a few hundred yards further along the right of the brigade. None of those shells came across where we were. While the cannonade was at its height, and of course such a cannonade as this is always the precursor of a charge of a line of battle, General Taylor said that he must have some orders from General Slocum's headquarters as he did not know what was wanted of him, so he said: "Grubb, ride to General Slocum's headquarters and ask him what he wants me to do." I had then one of the most terrible experiences that I ever had under artillery fire, and what is more, I had two of them, for I rode down that road across that line of firing, and I think I came nearer being killed by the flying pieces of fence rails and pieces of trees than by the shells. I found the oak tree, but I did not find General Slocum, and I came back to General Taylor, really very much bewildered by the terrible fire, and told him that General Slocum was not where he said. He merely said: "Go back and find him." And I had to do what I should have done, of course, at first. It must be remembered that I was only a little over nineteen years of age. I finally did find General Slocum more than half a mile from where I was told he would be, and a very heavy infantry fight going on in front of him. I told him what General Taylor had said. He did not even look at me but simply said: "When I want him I will let him know." Which I had the pleasure of repeating to General Taylor word for word. The last time I came down the road the cannonade had almost died out, and the infantry fighting about opposite to where I had seen General Slocum was very severe. The corps engaged, it turned out, was the Third Corps and the division on its left which was of course next to our right because we were right in front in column and had been marching south when we halted, was General Phil. Kearney's division and commanded by General Phil. Kearney in person. Now it will be seen that our brigade being in column of four right in front under the old tactics to have formed a line of battle the order would have been given front, and all the men would have turned to the left which would have brought their backs to the enemy, as the enemy was on our right or west side. To have formed the line of battle we would have had to have faced by the rear rank, and while that did not make much difference in merely forming the line, only so far as the file closers were concerned, any subsequent manoeuvers from that formation would become exceedingly complicated; and I doubt whether any of the regiments of the First Brigade at that time could have successfully performed those manoeuvers. These were some of the difficulties which the Upton's tactics subsequently adopted, aimed to obviate and did so.

General Kearney was the idol and hero of our brigade from the time we first saw him. He and all his staff were well known to every man and officer of us; and when Captain Moore of Kearney's staff came riding down the road waving his hat and calling out that General Kearney had lost a battery, and wanted the Jersey Brigade to help him get it back, it seemed to me that the whole brigade heard him because I am sure that no orders were given to do that which occurred, and I had barely time to scramble on my horse and join in the rushing throng. General Taylor called to me as I passed him: "Keep ahead of them and keep them from going too far. The enemy's line is in the woods right in front of our guns." Captain Moore, who was talking to him, had probably told him this. The guns that had been captured were not more than three hundred yards from us, a little advanced to the west of the road. I had noticed that they were not gone when I passed along on my ride to General Slocum's but the melee was so confused that I have not and never had a very clear idea of it. When I got to where the guns were the road was somewhat sunken and as the bank was so steep that I could not ride my horse up, I jumped off and scrambled up. There were a good many men among the guns before I got there, and the guns were being re-captured. But I do know that when I passed near a gun, a sergeant of the First Regiment, whose name was either Hollins or Hollister, had a Rebel prisoner by the neck. The man, though captured, had not surrendered, and as I passed him in carrying out the order which I had, to stop the men from going beyond the guns, he thrust at our sergeant with his bayonet, missed him, and gave me a prod, the scar of which I carry to this day. Though it did not disable me then or now, as it was on the inside of the thigh. I passed the order to halt to several of the officers of our brigade. It is my impression that there were lots of Kearney's men from his own division who were there almost instantly; but I do not think they were there when we first came up.

I expected that we would receive a withering volley from the woods which were only across a small field in which the General had told me the enemy would be. For some blessed reason that volley never came; and in a few minutes our men were re-called to the road and continued our march, and towards night fall we went into line of battle along the side of the road not more than twenty yards from the road side. On the west side our skirmishers were thrown out perhaps fifty yards more and we engaged with the Rebel skirmishers until dark. There was a good deal of artillery firing along the roads which intersected the road on which we were marching; but most of the shots went through the tree tops and only a few of our men were injured. The line we were holding and which we held there from dark until twelve o'clock that night was the gap in the line into which the enemy had charged and captured Major General McCall and a large part of his division.

About nine o'clock that night I, having been constantly engaged under General Taylor's orders, in passing along our skirmisher line and getting reports from the officers, came up to where the General was in a fence corner, and found him utterly exhausted. Neither he nor I had had any nourishment, except a cup of coffee for breakfast, since the night before and that coffee had been given to us by some of the men of our headquarters. The wagon with all our rations was with the train and we did not see it for thirty-six hours afterwards.

I said to him: "General, the brigade is very much mixed up and ought to be straightened out." He said: "Very vell, sir, go straighten it out." And so I went, but I had not gone more than twenty steps before I came to the conclusion that that was too much of a contract for a young man of my age, so I went to Colonel Torbert of the First Regiment and stated the case, just what the General had said, and that I believed that General Taylor was entirely exhausted, and that the job was too big for me. He said: "Never mind, sonny, I will fix it up for you." So we went together and Colonel Torbert arranged the brigade that night. Some of the companies of the Second were mixed up with the Third, and some of the Third were mixed up with the First until we straightened them out. The men were lying down, some of them asleep, all of them cross, and it was no easy job to shift them around, but we finally got it done about eleven o'clock. I got back to my old colored man, James Huggs, who had a blanket for me in the same fence corner where the General was, and I had about two hours' sound sleep. A little before one o'clock an aid of General Slocum's gave us marching orders. We found an entire brigade in the road ready to take our places, and passing through them to the road we continued our march in column going somewhere, we did not know where, but headed, we all knew, towards the James

River on the way from Richmond. This last fact was heartbreaking to the men, for from the moment that we landed at West Point in May our faces had been towards the Rebel Capitol. Although the battle of Gaines' Mills had been lost just the day after we were much nearer Richmond than we were now and it was only the night of the battle of Charles City crossroads that our men realized that we were retreating. We marched until about seven o'clock in the morning and then the brigade was given about three hours' rest along the road. The General and I had some coffee which the men of the Provost Guard gave us and I went down into my old Company C, of the Third Regiment, and got from Richard Poole, a private in that company, who was a painter in Burlington, three hard tack, and after he had given them to me, just one-half of all he had, I searched in my pocket and found the silver ten cent piece, that was the last thing I had. Richard refused to accept this in exchange for the hard tack, but I finally pressed it upon him as a souvenir, and he showed it to me many times afterwards. About twelve o'clock the brigade was assembled and marched along the road towards Malvern Hill which we did not then know by that name or any other name, but it was a high and commanding position and we saw a great many of our batteries already in position upon it, and very readily came to the conclusion that our army was going to make a stand there. I think the Jersey Brigade was at that time in the rear guard, and the reason I think so is because after our brigade passed through the pickets which were at the edge of the hill nothing came behind us but some cavalry, and I have a good reason to remember that. Within about a half a mile of the hill on the left hand side of the road was a fine farm and near the fence were two fine cherry trees full of cherries. As we passed along, the General and myself being in the rear of the brigade, he said: "I would like to have some of those very much." So I immediately said: "I will get you some." I got over the fence and climbed up a tree dropping my sword and belt in the clover at the foot of the tree as I went up, I broke off a good many branches and proceeded to fill myself as quickly as possible. A scouting party of some of our cavalry came by going toward the hill and an officer told the General that there were some Rebel scouts not very far behind him, upon which the General recalled me from the tree, and we proceeded to rejoin the brigade which had gone up Malvern Hill. When the brigade was halted and arranged upon the line which had been assigned to us near the top of the hill, I instantly noticed that I had not my sword and belt and remembered that they were in the grass at the foot of the cherry tree a half a mile outside of our lines. I asked the General for permission to go back and get them and he proceeded to read me a lecture on carelessness. Saying, among other things, which I distinctly remember and always have, that "A soldier should lose his head rather than his sword." So I went back to the picket line and very fortunately for me I happened to know the captain very well who commanded a cavalry troop that was on picket on that spot, that is to say, near the base of the hill. He said to me that he had not seen any Rebel scouts for half an hour and that he would send two of his men with me to get the sword which he did, and we all got back safely without seeing anybody, and the cavalry also got a lot of cherries. I mention this incident so particularly, because it has a very particular bearing upon a very extraordinary occurrence that happened that night. There was an immense park of our wagons not very far from the hill the night before the battle of Malvern Hill, and while the brigade was on the hill in line of battle and sleeping behind the breast works which they had made of logs and earth, a very flimsy sort of breast works, but which by reason of the admirable position on the hill would have been very effective if assaulted, General Taylor received an order informing him that the wagon trains of the army would be burnt that night, and he, accompanied by some others and my old servant, James Huggs, went down into the wagon park and took out a small quantity of their personal belongings, among other things a small hand bag of mine containng some underclothing, my mother's letters, and a few other things of that kind. I did not go with them as I was asleep at the root of a tree, and when the order came the General told my man he did not wish to disturb me. I saw the printed order the next morning. It was in the same form and apparently the same type as that which we received from the headquarters of the Army of the Potomac. General Taylor returned to where he had placed his headquarters under a great white pine tree, and my old servant, James Huggs, sat at the camp fire, for, although it had been a hot day, the nights were cool and the fire was lighted. Huggs says that about eleven o'clock while the General was walking up and down between the tree and the fire, the orderly on duty came up to the General and said that a messenger from General McClellan's headquarters wanted to see him outside of the rifle pit, and Huggs says that the General walked straight down that way, he, of course, not going with him. The next morning at grey day light, I awoke with the most intense gnawing hunger that I had ever experienced in my life. I had had nothing to eat but three hard tack, two cups of coffee, and some cherries for two days, and I had ridden probably fifty miles in those two days. I had, moreover, been in a pretty severe fight and had an ugly wound in my leg which hurt me every instant I sat in the saddle. As soon as I sat up and rubbed the sleep out of my eyes I saw within about twenty-five yards of me a small pig rooting along on the ground, I also saw right close to me a rifle of the orderly's leaning against the tree, it being the custom then for an orderly merely to have the ram rod in his hand while he was on duty. I knew there was a positive order against the discharge of any firearm without permission, but I was very hungry and there was the pig, so I took deliberate and careful aim, and killed that pig dead. Simultaneously with the crack of the rifle came the voice of General Taylor: "If you had missed him, sir, I would have put you under arrest." He was standing on the other side of the tree and had not lain down all night. The pig was cooked and eaten at once. The battle of Malvern Hill which took place that day was a magnificent pageant for those of our brigade who could see it. The coming down of a great mass of the enemy on the open plain to their utter destruction by the awful artillery fire. It was indeed a cruel and bloody sight, but after it was all over, many of us felt that we were avenged for what had happened at Gaines' Mills.

Those of us who can remember can even see today in our mind's eye, knapsack, hats, and even bodies of men thrown up in the air by the explosions of our shells in the serried masses of the enemy. Our brigade was not engaged at all, some men were hit by spent shots and bits of shells, but I think our casualties were twenty-eight in all. During the day on more than one occasion my attention was called to the fact that General Taylor was not wearing his own sword, but the sword that he was wearing belonged to his son, Captain Taylor, who had been partially disabled in the battle of Gaines' Mills. I noticed this because the two swords were not alike at all, and moreover, because I had been the object of a lesson on carelessness the previous afternoon, but of course I did not say anything.

The morning after the battle of Malvern Hill our brigade marched into a great wheat field at Brandon, near Harrison's Landing, and went into camp in the mud. As soon as the wagons were up and our tents were pitched, General Taylor directed me to mount my horse and accompany him. We went straight down to the James River and up along the river bank until we came to Berkley

Mansion, which was General McClellan's headquarters. We had an orderly with us and both dismounted and left our horses with the orderly. I accompanied the General into the house and upstairs to the second floor. There were a number of wounded men in the house lying on the floors, and the house was crowded with officers of all grades. General Taylor went into a room on the second floor which I afterwards found was General McClellan's private headquarters and in a few minutes came out and said to me. "I shall be here for some time, you may make yourself comfortable, and when I want you I will call you." So I went out of the house, for it was indeed a grewsome place. It was raining hard, and after telling the orderly to spread an oil cloth blanket, which I had, over my horse, I looked around for a place to make myself comfortable, and found a chicken coop with some bright dry straw on the floor (there were no chickens in it) so I lay down and went to sleep. In about an hour an orderly called me. The General was standing on the porch, mounting our horses we rode off towards camp, I riding, of course, a horse's length behind the General. After going about two or three hundred yards, he checked his horse and said: "Ride up along side of me." Which I did. He then said: "Did you notice that I did not have my sword when I went to General McClellan's headquarters?" I said: "I did, sir, I noticed that you had neither sword nor belt." He said: "You see I have got them now." I said: "I do, sir." He said: "Well, I got them at General McClellan's headquarters." He said: "Last night while you were asleep an orderly told me that a messenger from General McClellan wanted to see me outside the rifle pit, I went there and two men on gray horses met me, one of whom was dismounted. This man presented a pistol at my head and instantly demanded my sword. Believing that I was captured and a prisoner there was nothing else for me to do but give him my sword which I did. Upon taking it he immediately mounted his horse and rode off."

That is all that General Taylor ever told me on the subject, and it is all I know about it. (I may add that General McClellan's body guard always rode gray horses). The fact is that this occurred, on my word as a gentleman and a soldier, exactly as I have stated it.

As the brigade was marching in to the great wheat field at Berkley where the army was then commencing to encamp, suddenly and without any idea that the enemy was in the vicinity, several shells came in and exploded among the wagon trains which were in the road along side of which our men were marching. My recollection is that not more than a dozen shells came. A regiment of Zouaves, which I think were the 55th of New York, went back in double-quick, and I understood captured two guns which the enemy had run up close to our encampment without any supports whatever. The official records will show the circumstances of this. I remember that one of the shells exploded within a few feet of General Taylor's horse.

Some incidents of interest occurred during our encampment at Malvern Hill. It was hot and uncomfortable and sorrowful, for there were many deaths and bands playing the Dead March were continually heard through the day. Deaths from sickness and many wounded.

One night, a few nights after we encamped, we were roused at midnight by a very lively cannonade from the opposite side of the river. Our camp was about a quarter of a mile back from the river, the long roll was beaten throughout the army and the brigade turned out and stood in line. I do not think there were any casualties in the brigade though there were some in our division from its shells. One man I remember as Dr. Oakley asked me to go and see a man in the field hospital who had his entire stomach carried away by shells and lived four days afterwards. This wound is reported among the curiosities of the war. I saw the man twice and strange to say, he appeared to be suffering no pain except through hunger.

A few days after our arrival at the Camp, President Lincoln came down and reviewed the army. I presume by reason of the small space in which it was necessary to hold it each brigade was drawn up on the northern side of its own camp in double columns, closed en masse, and the field officers were dismounted. My clothing, all except the one suit which I had during the seven days' battle, had been lost and it happened that the only coat I had was a short jacket coming to the waist, and the only trousers I had were those which I had worn since the 27th of June. My saddle had been hit twice with pieces of shell, once while I was in it and once when I was not. It was not torn much but the screws were all loosened in it and one of them had worked up and from day to day had torn my trousers to such an extent that I can only say they were not fit to appear in review; so upon seeing my condition General Taylor excused me from going in the review and I sat in the door of my tent next to General Taylor's and within a few feet of it. President Lincoln rode a large bay horse and was dressed in a black frock coat and a high silk hat and rode at the head of the cavalcade with General McClellan and his staff of probably a hundred officers immediately behind him. They passed down from east to west along the front of the army, the President taking off his hat as he passed the colors of each brigade. When they arrived in front of our brigade they halted and General Taylor and the President came up to General Taylor's tent, no others were with them. The President dismounted and my servant, James Huggs, who is still living, brought camp stools and they sat down under the fly of General Taylor's tent; it seems that the President wanted a drink of water, the day being very hot. James Huggs went to the spring a few yards away and got some water and the President drank heartily of it; as he got up to go away he saw me standing in the position of a soldier facing him at my tent door and he said to General Taylor: "I suppose this is one of your staff, I hope that he has not been wounded?" General Taylor called me to them and told him that I was Captain Grubb on his staff, and told one or two very pleasant things about me to the President which caused my cheeks to tingle and then taking me by the shoulder, he said: "He would have been in the review but his clothes were not good enough to allow him." President Lincoln put his hand on my shoulder, I shall never forget the kind expression of his magnificent eyes, as he looked me in the face and said: "My son, I think your country can afford to give you a new pair of breeches." As these were the only words that President Lincoln ever said to me they impressed themselves very deeply on my mind. I have never forgotten them and never shall.

The rest of our stay at Harrison's Landing is filled with unpleasant memories for me. I had contracted typhoid fever although I did not know it and tried to fight it off, and did so until the morning the brigade marched from Harrison's Landing when in the wind and dust of that morning I mounted my brown stallion with great difficulty, fell over the other side of him into the dust and the next thing I remember was awaking up in New York Harbor in the hospital ship some ten days afterwards with two Sisters of Mercy taking care of me and my old servant, James Huggs, standing at the foot of the bed. He had hired a colored man whom he found and helped him carry me down to the water's edge and succeeded in getting me on board the hospital ship "Spaulding" in a little dug out canoe, for the anchor of that ship had been raised and she was the last hospital ship to leave filled with sick and wounded.

I did not know that the brigade had been most dreadfully cut up and General Taylor killed at the Bull Run Bridge until after I had been sent from the hospital ship to my father's house in Burlingtou, where I found a letter from Colonel Torbert commanding the brigade and asking me to serve on his staff. I joined the brigade just before the Crampton's Pass battle (and my account of that which I delivered at a reunion of the brigade at my place, Edgewater Park, printed at their request I herewith enclose).

We saw the battle of Antietam and were under a terrible artillery fire but we were in the reserve and I am sure that I need only say that it was the opinion of every man and officer in our brigade that if the Sixth Corps had been thrown forward that afternoon over the Burnside bridge after Burnside crossed it and placed across the right flank of the Confederate army, which were all there lying in the wheat field opposite us, the result of that battle would have been far different from what it was.

After Antietam we marched to Bakersville and encamped there and were there joined by the Twenty-third New Jersey Regiment, into which I was promoted as Major a few days before the battle of Fredericksburg. (And I would suggest that as the history of that regiment which, of course, is part of the history of the brigade, has been carefully collected and printed by the Regimental Association of the Twenty-third Regiment, and that regiment was in that brigade until the expiration of its term of service in June, 1863, and in battle with the brigade in the battles of Fredericksburg and Salem Church, that that printed history be received as part of the history of the brigade.)

E. BURD GRUBB.

The Episode of the Surgeon of the Third Regiment

The surgeon of the 3rd New Jersey Regiment was appointed by Governor Olden about ten days after the regiment arrived in Camp Olden. His name was Lorenzo Louis Cox, he was a man about twenty-five years of age. He had a fine appearance, well educated and an excellent surgeon. He was a grandson of Mr. Redmond Cox of Philadelphia, a member of a well known family. Redmond Cox was an intimate friend of my father, but my father had nothing whatever to do with the appointment of Dr. Cox, and did not know of it until after it was made.

After the battle of Bull Run, and during the early autumn the Third Regiment was engaged in erecting Fort Worth, one of the defences of Washington, about a mile west of Alexandria Seminary. Probably the uncovering of so much fresh earth which had to be done in erecting the Fort, which was quite a large one, caused an outbreak of malarial fever, most of it ordinary chills and fever. The sick call was sounded at half-past six every morning and a very large proportion of the regiment filed up to Dr. Cox's tent and received a drink of whiskey and some quinine pills. Those of the Third Regiment who read this will probably remember two very ridiculous occurences in this connection. Dr. Cox had an Irishman who was a private in one of the companies and he was his assistant. The Doctor had a barrel of whiskey in his tent from which he served the rations every morning; he noticed that this whiskey became exhausted more rapidly than in his opinion it should, he therefore poured into the whiskey barrel a very large quantity of quinine, and the consequence was that the next morning his man Patrick was so drunk that he had to be taken down to the creek to be soused to bring him to, and he could not hear for two or three days.

The other occurrence was that one morning on guard mount the Adjutant, whose name was Fairliegh, (an Englishman and the youngest son of Lord Fairliegh), appeared on his horse, which was a light bay and which had been striped with white paint on the ribs during the night and every hair on his tail shaved off. It transpired at the regimental court-martial that Dr. Cox's Patrick was very largely responsible for the damage to the Adjutant's horse. During the months of August and September and also during the whole winter of 1861-1862 the First New Jersey Brigade picketed in front of their lines, and during August and September these pickets were not very far from and in front of Alexandria, not more than three miles at the utmost. The enemy's pickets were very close to ours and a number of skirmishes along the Little River turn pike and the corn fields adjacent thereto occurred. Gradually our picket lines were advanced until, about the latter part of September, we took in Mrs. Fitzhugh's plantation and picketed almost up to Annandale. Dr. Cox and his assistant were out along the picket lines almost every afternoon. Many of the men would be ailing and there was an occasional gun-shot wound that would have to be looked after. Dr. Cox rode a very handsome cream-colored mule, and Patrick had an army horse, Patrick carried the knap-sack of medical stores and surgical instruments strapped on his back. One afternoon Dr. Cox, who had visited Mrs. Fitzhugh's plantation several times, and it was at that time a little outside of our picket lines, started to go there again, when he was pounced upon by six of the Louden scouts, Confederate Cavalry, and, although he tried to make his mule run away from them he could not do so and was captured, Patrick jumped off his horse and ran into the woods and succeeded in getting back into our lines with his medical knap-sack. He reported Dr. Cox killed as there had been several pistol shots fired, Cox was not armed. On the evening of the next day, Dr. Cox returned to the camp of the Third Regiment and reported the facts about as I have related them here to Colonel Taylor, and also to all of the officers of the regiment who were his friends and who were interested in the occurrence. He told us that he had been taken to Mannassas Junction and had been for some time in the tent of General Joseph E. Johnson, the commander of the Rebel Army that then faced us. Everybody was glad of his release which was of course because of his being a non-combattant. He resumed his duties and I do not remember that the incident was spoken of again in the regiment until the following very curious occurrence took place.

When the army advanced on Mannassas Junction in March, 1862, the Third New Jersey Regiment was in the extreme front.

The skirmishers of that regiment captured a train of cars loaded with provisions, and were also the first in the Rebel encampment at Mannassas. Some of the members of the regiment entered General Joseph E. Johnson's tent, which had been evacuated so suddenly that a number of his papers and his military sash were left which these men obtained. They naturally examined the papers and were surprised to find a report taken down by a member of General Johnson's staff of the conversation had with Dr. Cox of the Third New Jersey Volunteers. This report stated that Dr. Cox had given General Johnson all the information regarding the troops at and around Alexandria that he desired and that he Cox had particularly stated the number of men which General Montgomery commanded at Alexandria. Fortunately for Cox, the aid stated this number at 10,000, which was what Cox did say, and which was twice as many as Montgomery had. These papers were forwarded to Washington, whether through the headquarters of the regiment or not, I do not know, but a few days after that a squad of the United States Cavalry came to the Third Regiment and the officer in command arrested Dr. Cox and took him to Washington where he was immediately incarcerated in the old Capitol Prison. He remained there for a very considerable time, my impression is for several months. I wrote to my father in regard to this and he went to Washington and had an interview with Edward M. Stanton who was then Secretary of War, Mr. Stanton had been my father's counsel before the war in Lancaster and was an intimate friend of his. He had great trouble to get Mr. Stanton to take the matter up at all, but when he finally did, Cox was found to be innocent, but foolish. He returned to the regiment but only for a few days. The men, and a number of the officers would not receive him, and he resigned and took a position as surgeon of one of the Pacific Mail Steamers in which position he contracted the chargres fever and died. The occurrence was a very sad one. Cox was entirely innocent. He was a perfectly loyal and true man. He was one of the very best surgeons in the army at that time and almost certainly would have had a brilliant career. His military life was cut short, and probably his actual life also from having talked too much. He told me himself, that, in the interview in General Johnson's tent he had purposely given him all the false information that he could think of, and that he had purposely stated Montgomery's troops to be twice their actual strength.

  The correspondence in regard to this will be found in the official record, see general index, page 211, Lewis L. Cox 13845.

I have read the correspondence, but the volume in which it is, I do not now find in my collection.

E. BURD GRUBB.

I was First Lieutenant of Co. D, 3d N. J. Vols., and Aide de Camp on the staff of Brig. General George W. Taylor, First New Jersey Brigade, during this campaign.

E. BURD GRUBB.